Scruffy Runs

Story by Annette Smith
Photography by Lindsay Edwards

Rigby®

A Harcourt Achieve Imprint

www.Rigby.com
1-800-531-5015

Dad said to Josh,
"I'm going for a run
down by the river."

"Can I come with you?"
said Josh.
"Can Scruffy come, too?"

Scruffy jumped up at Josh.

Dad laughed.

"Yes," he said.

"You can ride your bike,
and Scruffy can come, too.
But he will have to be a good dog
and not run away."

Down by the river,
Dad ran slowly at first.

Scruffy ran slowly, too.
And Josh went slowly on his bike.

Then Scruffy ran very fast.

He went so fast
that he got away from Dad.

"Come back here, Scruffy,"
shouted Dad.
"**Come back here now!**"

But Scruffy did not come back.

"Dad, I will get him for you,"
said Josh.
"I can go very fast on my bike."

Josh went after Scruffy.

"Scruffy! Scruffy!" shouted Josh.
"Come here to me."

Scruffy looked back at Josh.

"Sit, Scruffy! **Sit!**" shouted Josh.

Scruffy sat down on the path.

Josh jumped off his bike.

"I got you, Scruffy!" he said.
"Stay here with me.
Here comes Dad."

"Josh," laughed Dad,

"**you** will have to look after Scruffy.

He is too naughty for me."